U.S. Department of Justice
Office of Justice Programs
National Institute of Justice

National Institute of Justice
Law Enforcement and Corrections Standards and Testing Program

An Introduction to Biological Agent
Detection Equipment for
Emergency First Responders

NIJ Guide 101–00

December 2001

U.S. Department of Justice
Office of Justice Programs
810 Seventh Street N.W.
Washington, DC 20531

John Ashcroft
Attorney General

Deborah J. Daniels
Assistant Attorney General

Sarah V. Hart
Director, National Institute of Justice

For grant and funding information, contact:
Department of Justice Response Center
800–421–6770

Office of Justice Programs
World Wide Web Site
http://www.ojp.usdoj.gov

National Institute of Justice
World Wide Web Site
http://www.ojp.usdoj.gov/nij

U.S. Department of Justice
Office of Justice Programs
National Institute of Justice

An Introduction to Biological Agent Detection Equipment for Emergency First Responders

NIJ Guide 101–00

Dr. Alim A. Fatah[1]
John A. Barrett[2]
Richard D. Arcilesi, Jr.[2]
Dr. Kenneth J. Ewing[2]
Charlotte H. Lattin[2]
LTC Timothy F. Moshier[3]

Coordination by:
Office of Law Enforcement Standards
National Institute of Standards and Technology
Gaithersburg, MD 20899

Prepared for:
National Institute of Justice
Office of Science and Technology
Washington, DC 20531

December 2001

NCJ 190747

[1]National Institute of Standards and Technology, Office of Law Enforcement Standards.

[2]Battelle Memorial Institute.

[3]Joint Program Office for Biological Defense (JPOBD).

National Institute of Justice

Sarah V. Hart
Director

This guide was prepared for the National Institute of Justice, U.S. Department of Justice, by the Office of Law Enforcement Standards of the National Institute of Standards and Technology under Interagency Agreement 94–IJ–R–004, Project No. 99–060–CBW. It was also prepared under CBIAC contract No. SPO–900–94–D–0002 and Interagency Agreement M92361 between NIST and the Department of Defense Technical Information Center (DTIC).

The authors wish to thank Ms. Kathleen Higgins of the National Institute of Standards and Technology, Mr. Bill Haskell of SBCCOM, Ms. Priscilla S. Golden of General Physics, LTC Don Buley of the Joint Program Office of Biological Defense, Ms. Nicole Trudel of Camber Corporation, Dr. Stephen Morse of Centers for Disease Control, and Mr. Todd Brethauer of the Technical Support Working Group for their significant contributions to this effort. We would also like to acknowledge the Interagency Board for Equipment Standardization and Interoperability, which consists of Government and first responder representatives.

FOREWORD

The Office of Law Enforcement Standards (OLES) of the National Institute of Standards and Technology (NIST) furnishes technical support to the National Institute of Justice (NIJ) program to support law enforcement and criminal justice in the United States. OLES's function is to develop standards and conduct research that will assist law enforcement and criminal justice agencies.

OLES is: (1) subjecting existing equipment to laboratory testing and evaluation, and (2) conducting research leading to the development of several series of documents, including national standards, user guides, and technical reports.

This document covers research conducted by OLES under the sponsorship of NIJ. Additional reports as well as other documents are being issued under the OLES program in the areas of protective clothing and equipment, communications systems, emergency equipment, investigative aids, security systems, vehicles, weapons, and analytical techniques and standard reference materials used by the forensic community.

Technical comments and suggestions concerning this guide are invited from all interested parties. They may be addressed to the Office of Law Enforcement Standards, National Institute of Standards and Technology, 100 Bureau Drive, Stop 8102, Gaithersburg, MD 20899–8102.

Sarah V. Hart, Director
National Institute of Justice

CONTENTS

TABLES

FIGURES

COMMONLY USED SYMBOLS AND ABBREVIATIONS

A	ampere	hf	high frequency	o.d.	outside diameter
ac	alternating current	Hz	hertz	Ω	ohm
AM	amplitude modulation	i.d.	inside diameter	p.	page
cd	candela	in	inch	Pa	pascal
cm	centimeter	IR	infrared	pe	probable error
CP	chemically pure	J	joule	pp.	pages
c/s	cycle per second	L	lambert	ppm	parts per million
d	day	L	liter	qt	quart
dB	decibel	lb	pound	rad	radian
dc	direct current	lbf	pound-force	rf	radio frequency
°C	degree Celsius	lbf·in	pound-force inch	rh	relative humidity
°F	degree Fahrenheit	lm	lumen	s	second
dia	diameter	ln	logarithm (base e)	SD	standard deviation
emf	electromotive force	log	logarithm (base 10)	sec.	Section
eq	equation	M	molar	SWR	standing wave ratio
F	farad	m	meter	uhf	ultrahigh frequency
fc	footcandle	μ	micron	UV	ultraviolet
fig.	Figure	min	minute	V	volt
FM	frequency modulation	mm	millimeter	vhf	very high frequency
ft	foot	mph	miles per hour	W	watt
ft/s	foot per second	m/s	meter per second	λ	wavelength
g	acceleration	mo	month	wk	week
g	gram	N	newton	wt	weight
gr	grain	N·m	newton meter	yr	year
H	henry	nm	nanometer		
h	hour	No.	number		

area=unit^2 (e.g., ft^2, in^2, etc.); volume=unit^3 (e.g., ft^3, m^3, etc.)

ACRONYMS SPECIFIC TO THIS DOCUMENT

APS	Aerosol Particle Sizer	IND	Investigational New Drug
BA	Biological Agent	IR	Infrared
BAWS	Biological Aerosol Warning System	JSLSCAD	Joint Service Lightweight Standoff Chemical Agent Detector
BDG	Bi-Diffractive Grating	LANL	Los Alamos National Laboratory
BW	Biological Warfare	LD$_{50}$	Lethal Dose for 50% of Population
CA	Chemical Agent	LIDAR	Light Detection and Ranging
CBMS	Chemical Biological Mass Spectrometer	LLNL	Lawrence Livermore National Laboratory
CIBADS	Canadian Integrated Biological Agent Detection System	MALDI-TOF	Matrix Assisted Laser Desorption Ionization-Time of Flight
CW	Chemical Warfare	mg	Milligram
DARPA	Defense Advanced Research Projects Agency	NASA	National Aeronautical Space Administration
DNA	Deoxyribonucleic Acid	PCR	Polymerase Chain Reaction
DoD BSK	Department of Defense Biological Sampling Kit	PHTLAAS	Portable High-Throughput Liquid Aerosol Air Sampler System
DOE	Department of Energy	PY-GC-IMS	Pyrolysis-Gas Chromatography-Ion Mobility Specrometer
ECBC	Edgewood Chemical and Biological Command	RNA	Ribonucleic Acid
EOO	Electro Optics Organization, Inc.	RSCAAL	Remote Sensing Chemical Agent Alarm
FLAPS	Fluorescent Aerodynamic Particle Sizer	SBCCOM	Soldier and Biological Chemical Command
FTIR	Fourier Transform Infrared	SESI	Science and Engineering Services, Inc.
HHA	Hand-Held Immunochromatographic Assay	SRI	Stanford Research Institute
HeNe	Helium-Neon	TE	Transverse Electric
HUS	Hemolytic uremic syndrome	TIMs	Toxic Industrial Materials
HVAPS	High Volume Aerodynamic Particle Sizer	TM	Transverse Magnetic
IAB	Interagency Board	TTP	Thrombocytopenic purpura
IBADS	Interim Biological Agent Detector System	UAV	Unmanned Aerial Vehicle
IMS	Ionization/Ion Mobility Spectrometry	WMD	Weapons of Mass Destruction

PREFIXES (See ASTM E380)

d	deci (10^{-1})	da	deka (10)
c	centi (10^{-2})	h	hecto (10^{2})
m	milli (10^{-3})	k	kilo (10^{3})
μ	micro (10^{-6})	M	mega (10^{6})
n	nano (10^{-9})	G	giga (10^{9})
p	pico (10^{-12})	T	tera (10^{12})

COMMON CONVERSIONS

0.30480 m = 1 ft	4.448222 N = 1 lbf
25.4 mm = 1 in	1.355818 J = 1 ft·lbf
0.4535924 kg = 1 lb	0.1129848 N m = 1 lbf·in
0.06479891g = 1gr	14.59390 N/m = 1 lbf/ft
0.9463529 L = 1 qt	6894.757 Pa = 1 lbf/in^2
3600000 J = 1 kW·hr	1.609344 km/h = 1 mph

psi = mm of Hg x (1.9339×10^{-2})

mm of Hg = psi x 51.71

Temperature: $T_C = (T_F - 32) \times 5/9$

Temperature: $T_F = (T_C \times 9/5) + 32$

ABOUT THIS GUIDE

The National Institute of Justice (NIJ) is the focal point for providing support to State and local law enforcement agencies in the development of counterterrorism technology and standards, including technological needs for chemical and biological defense. In recognizing the needs of State and local emergency first responders, the Office of Law Enforcement Standards (OLES) at the National Institute of Standards and Technology (NIST), working with NIJ, the Technical Support Working Group (TSWG), the U.S. Army Soldier and Biological Chemical Command (SBCCOM), and the Interagency Board for Equipment Standardization and Interoperability (IAB), is developing chemical and biological defense equipment guides. The guides will focus on chemical and biological equipment in areas of detection, personal protection, decontamination, and communication. This document focuses specifically on assisting the emergency first responder community in the understanding of biological agent detection equipment.

The long range plans are to: (1) subject existing biological agent detection equipment to laboratory testing and evaluation against a specified protocol, and (2) conduct research leading to the development of multiple series of documents, including national standards, user guides, and technical reports. It is anticipated that the testing, evaluation, and research processes will take several years to complete; therefore, NIJ has developed this initial guide for the emergency first responder community in order to facilitate an understanding of biological agent detection equipment.

In conjunction with this program, additional guides, as well as other documents, are being issued in the areas of chemical agent and toxic industrial material detection equipment, decontamination equipment, personal protective equipment, and communications equipment used in conjunction with protective clothing and respiratory equipment.

The information contained in this guide on specific equipment and technologies has been obtained through literature searches and market surveys. *Reference herein to any specific commercial products, processes, or services by trade name, trademark, manufacturer, or otherwise does not necessarily constitute or imply its endorsement, recommendation, or favoring by the United States Government. The information and statements contained in this guide shall not be used for the purposes of advertising, nor to imply the endorsement or recommendation of the United States Government.*

With respect to information provided in this guide, neither the United States Government nor any of its employees make any warranty, expressed or implied, including but not limited to the warranties of merchantability and fitness for a particular purpose. Further, neither the United States Government nor any of its employees assume any legal liability or responsibility for the accuracy, completeness, or usefulness of any information, apparatus, product, or process disclosed.

Technical comments, suggestions, and product updates are encouraged from interested parties. They may be addressed to the Office of Law Enforcement Standards, National Institute of Standards and Technology, 100 Bureau Drive, Stop 8102, Gaithersburg, MD 20899–8102. It is anticipated that this guide will be updated periodically.

AN INTRODUCTION TO BIOLOGICAL AGENT DETECTION EQUIPMENT FOR EMERGENCY FIRST RESPONDERS

The end of the cold war has reduced international tension between the super powers. However, ironically enough, this has resulted in regional instability due to a resurgence of nationalistic, religious, and ethnic strife, which presents a real threat to peace in all regions of the globe. Additionally, there has been a remarkable increase in the production and availability of chemical and biological weapons throughout the world. The combination of these factors has significantly increased the possibility of an attack on the United States involving the use of such weapons. Biological agents are often considered to be psychologically the more threatening of the two, and therefore provide more appeal to the terrorist.

Biological agents can be manufactured in facilities that are inexpensive to construct; that resemble pharmaceutical, food, or medical production sites; and that provide no detectable sign that such agents are being produced. One characteristic of biological agents that makes them so attractive to potential users is their remarkably low effective dose; that is, the mass of agent that is required to create the desired effect (incapacitation or death) on the target population. Figure 1 shows the approximate mass in milligrams (mg) of an agent needed to achieve the desired result in comparison to toxins and chemical agents. The mass of a paper clip is included in this diagram as a point of reference. The reader can immediately see the vast differences in effectiveness between biological agents (microbial agents, e.g., bacteria and viruses) and chemical agents. At the extreme, some biological agents are as much as 14 *billion* times more effective than chemical agents, making it easy to see why biological agents are often described as the poor man's atomic bomb. The reader should also note that if a terrorist chooses to use a toxin agent (in order to get relatively rapid effects in a tactical situation), a much greater mass of the toxin agent will have to be employed than if biological agents were being used. This mass of toxin agent in some cases may be equivalent to chemical agent masses.

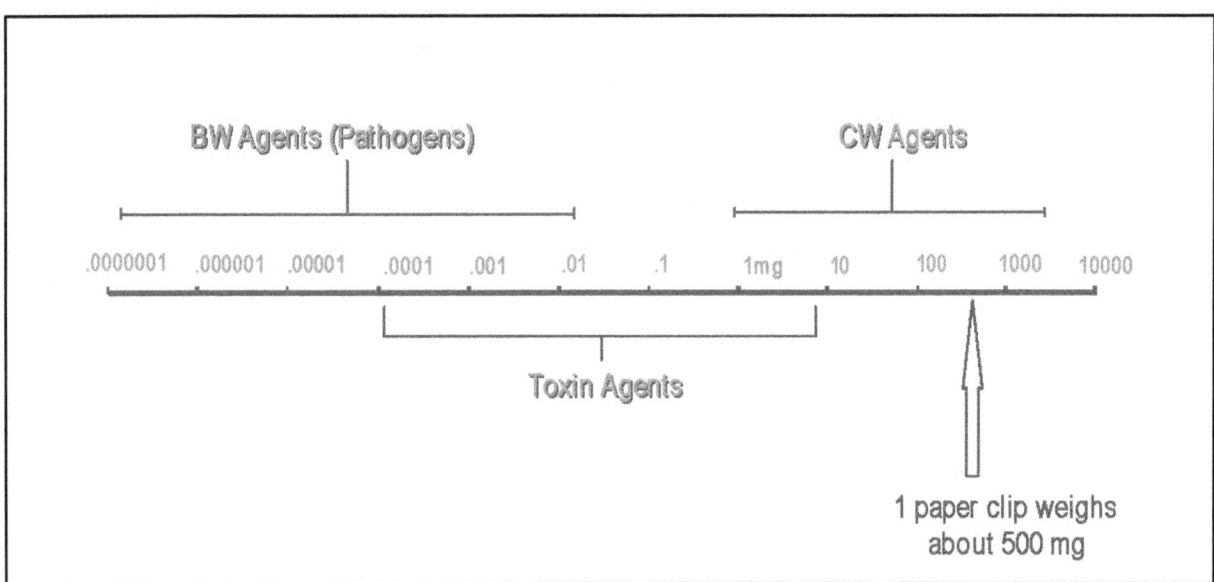

Figure 1. Comparative toxicity of effective doses of biological agents, toxins, and chemical agents

1. INTRODUCTION

The primary purpose of this document is to function as a guide and provide emergency first responders with information to aid them in their understanding of biological agent detection equipment.

This document is divided into seven sections and includes two appendices. Section 2 presents a review of biological agents. Specifically, it discusses the four most common classes of biological agents and provides information that includes epidemiology, symptoms, and treatment. Section 3 provides an overview of the known challenges associated with biological agent detection. Specifically, this section discusses general detection requirements such as ambient environment, selectivity, sensitivity, and sampling. Section 4 provides the reader with background information on the components of biological detection systems. Section 5 discusses known detection technologies, identified as point, standoff, or active standoff detection. Section 6 provides the emergency first responder with information on how to prepare for a biological incident. Section 7 concludes by providing a concise summary of the current state of biological agent detection. Appendix A identifies the sources of information used in developing this document. Appendix B provides contact information (telephone numbers and internet addresses) for State public health laboratories.

2. REVIEW OF BIOLOGICAL AGENTS

This section provides a description of the biological agents likely to be used in a terrorist attack. There are four categories under discussion: bacterial agents (sec. 2.1), viral agents (sec. 2.2), rickettsiae (sec. 2.3), and biological toxins (sec. 2.4).

2.1 Bacterial Agents

Bacteria are small, single-celled organisms, most of which can be grown on solid or in liquid culture media. Under special circumstances, some types of bacteria can transform into spores that are more resistant to cold, heat, drying, chemicals, and radiation than the bacterium itself. Most bacteria do not cause disease in human beings, but those that do cause disease act in two differing mechanisms: by invading the tissues or by producing poisons (toxins). Many bacteria, such as anthrax, have properties that make them attractive as potential warfare agents:

- Retained potency during growth and processing to the end product (biological weapon).
- Long "shelf-life."
- Low biological decay as an aerosol.

Other bacteria require stabilizers to improve their potential for use as biological weapons. Table 2–1 lists some of the common bacterial agents along with possible methods of dissemination, incubation period, symptoms, and treatment.

2.2 Viral Agents

Viruses are the simplest type of microorganism and consist of a nucleocapsid protein coat containing genetic material, either RNA or DNA. Because viruses lack a system for their own metabolism, they require living hosts (cells of an infected organism) for replication. As biological agents, they are attractive because many do not respond to antibiotics. However, their incubation periods are normally longer than for other biological agents, so incapacitation of victims may be delayed. Table 2–2 lists the common viral agents along with possible methods of dissemination, incubation period, symptoms, and treatment.

2.3 Rickettsiae

Rickettsiae are obligate intracellular bacteria that are intermediate in size between most bacteria and viruses and possess certain characteristics common to both bacteria and viruses. Like bacteria, they have metabolic enzymes and cell membranes, use oxygen, and are susceptible to broad-spectrum antibiotics, but like viruses, they grow only in living cells. Most rickettsiae can be spread only through the bite of infected insects and are not spread through human contact. Table 2–3 lists the common rickettsiae along with possible methods of dissemination, incubation periods, symptoms, and treatment.

2.4 Biological Toxins

Biological toxins are poisons produced by living organisms. It is the poison, not the organism, that produces harmful effects in man. A toxin typically develops naturally in a host organism (for example, saxitoxin is produced by marine algae); however, genetically altered and/or synthetically manufactured toxins have been produced in a laboratory environment. Biological toxins are most similar to chemical agents in their dissemination and effectiveness. Table 2–4 lists the common biological toxins along with possible methods of dissemination, incubation period, symptoms, and treatment.

Table 2–1. Bacterial agents

Biological Agent/Disease	Anthrax	Brucellosis	E. coli serotype (O157:H7)	Tularemia	Cholera
Likely Method of Dissemination	1. Spores in aerosol 2. Sabotage (food)	1. Aerosol 2. Sabotage (food)	Water and food supply contamination	1. Aerosol 2. Rabbits or ticks	1. Sabotage (food and water) 2. Aerosol
Transmissible Person to Person	No (except cutaneous)	Unknown	Unknown, evidence passed person-to-person in day-care or nursing homes	No	Rare
Incubation Period	1 d to 43 d	1 wk to 3 wk, sometimes months	Unknown	2 d to 10 d	3 d to 5 d
Duration of Illness	3 d to 5 d (usually fatal)	Unknown	5 d to 10 d (most cases)	>2 wk	>1 wk
Lethality	Contact or cutaneous anthrax: fatality rate of 5 % to 20 % Inhalational anthrax: after symptoms appear almost always fatal, regardless of treatment	Low	0 % to 15 % if develop hemolytic uremic syndrome (HUS); 5 % if develop thrombotic thrombocytopenic purpura (TTP)	Moderate if left untreated	Low (<1 %) with treatment; high (>50 %) without
Vaccine Efficacy (for aerosol exposure)/ Antitoxin	Currently no human data	Vaccine under evaluation	No vaccine	No commercially available vaccine	No data on aerosol
Symptoms and Effects	Flu-like, upper-respiratory distress; fever and shock in 3 d to 5 d, followed by death	Irregular prolonged fever, profuse sweating, chills, joint and muscle pain, persistent fatigue	Gastrointestinal (diarrhea, vomiting) dehydration; in severe cases, cardiac arrest and death, HUS, or TTP	Chills; sustained fever; prostration; tendency for pneumonia; enlarged, painful lymph nodes; headache; malaise; anorexia; nonproductive cough	Sudden onset with nausea, vomiting, diarrhea, rapid dehydration, toxemia and collapse
Treatment	Vaccine available for cutaneous, possibly inhalation, anthrax. Cutaneous anthrax responds to antibiotics (penicillin, terramycin, chloromycetin), sulfadiazine, and immune serum. Pulmonary (inhaled) anthrax responds to immune serum in initial stages but is little use after disease is well established. Intestinal, same as for pulmonary	Antibiotics	Antibiotics available; most recover without antibiotics within 5 d to 10 d; do not use antidiarrheal agents	Vaccination using live attenuated organisms reduces severity and transmittability; antibiotics (streptomycin, aureomycin, chloromycetin, doxycycline, tetracycline, and chloramphenical)	Replenish fluids and electrolytes; antibiotics (tetracycline, ciprofloxicin, and erythromycin) enhance effectiveness of rehydration and reduce organism in body
Potential as Biological Agent	High, Iraqi and USSR biological programs worked to develop anthrax as a bio-weapon	Unknown	Unknown	High, if delivered via aerosol form (highly infectious, 90 % to 100 %)	Not appropriate for aerosol delivery

Table 2–1. Bacterial agents–Continued

Biological Agent/Disease	Diphtheria	Glanders	Melioidosis	Plague (Bubonic and Pneumonic)	Typhoid Fever
Likely Method of Dissemination	Unknown	1. Aerosol 2. Cutaneous	1. Food contamination (rodent feces) 2. Inhalation 3. Insect bites 4. Direct contact with infected animals	1. Infected fleas (Bubonic and Pneumonic) 2. Aerosol (Pneumonic)	1. Contact with infected person 2. Contact with contaminated substances
Transmissible Person to Person	High	High	No	High (Pneumonic)	High
Incubation Period	2 d to 5 d	3 d to 5 d	Days	1 d to 3 d	7 d to 14 d
Duration of Illness	Unknown	Unknown	4 d to 20 d	1 d to 6 d (usually fatal)	Unknown
Lethality	5 % to 10 % fatality	50 % to 70 %	Variable	5 % to 10 % if treated **Bubonic: 30 % to 75 % if untreated** Pneumonic: 95 % if untreated	<1 % if treated; 10 % to 14 % if untreated
Vaccine Efficacy (for aerosol exposure)/ Antitoxin	DPT vaccine 85 % effective; booster recommended every 10 yr	No vaccine	No vaccine	Vaccine not available	Oral vaccine (Vivotif) and single dose injectable vaccine (capsular poly-saccharide antigen); both vaccines are equally effective and offer 65 % to 75 % protection against the disease
Symptoms and Effects	Local infection usually in respiratory passages; delay in treatment can cause damage to heart, kidneys, and central nervous system	Skin lesions, ulcers in skin, mucous membranes, and viscera; if inhaled, upper respiratory tract involvement	Cough, fever, chills, muscle/joint pain, nausea, and vomiting; progressing to death	Enlarged lymph nodes in groin; septicemic (spleen, lungs, meninges affected)	Prolonged fever, lymph tissue involvement; ulceration of intestines; enlargement of spleen; rose-colored spots on skin; constipation or diarrhea
Treatment	Antitoxin extremely effective; antibiotic (penicillin) shortens the duration of illness	Drug therapy (streptomycin and sulfadiazine) is somewhat effective	Antibiotics (doxycycline, chlorothenicol, tetracycline) and sulfadiazine	Doxycycline (100 mg 2x/d for 7 d); ciprofloxicin also effective	Antibiotics (amoxicillin or cotrimoxazole) shorten period of communicability and cure disease rapidly
Potential as Biological Agent	Very low—symptoms not severe enough to incapacitate; rare cases of severe infection	Unknown	Moderate—rare disease, no vaccine available	High—highly infectious, particularly in pneumonic (aerosol) form; lack of stability and loss of virulence complicate its use	Not likely to be deployed via aerosol; more likely for covert contamination of water or food

Table 2–2. Viral agents

Biological Agent/Disease	Marburg Virus	Junin Virus	Rift Valley Fever Virus	Smallpox	Venezuelan Equine Encephalitis
Likely Method of Dissemination	Aerosol	Epidemiology not known	Mosquito-borne; in biological scenario, aerosols or droplets	Aerosol	1. Aerosol 2. Infected vectors
Transmissible Person to Person	Unknown	Unknown	Unknown	High	No
Incubation Period	5 d to 7 d	7 d to 16 d	2 d to 5 d	10 d to 12 d	1 d to 6 d
Duration of Illness	Unknown	16 d	2 d to 5 d	4 wk	Days to weeks
Lethality	25 %	18 %	<1 %	20 % to 40 % (Viriole major) <1 % (Viriole minor)	1 % to 60 %
Vaccine Efficacy (for aerosol exposure)/ Antitoxin	No vaccine	No vaccine	Inactivated vaccine available in limited quantities	Vaccine protects against infection within 3 d to 5 d of exposure	Experimental only: TC–83 protects against 30 LD_{50}s to 500 LD_{50}s in hamsters
Symptoms and Effects	Sudden onset of fever, malaise, muscle pain, headache, and conjunctivitis, followed by sore throat, vomiting, diarrhea, rash, and both internal and external bleeding (begins 5th day). Liver function may be abnormal and platelet function may be impaired.	Hemorrhagic syndrome, chills, sweating, exhaustion and stupor	Febrile illness, sometimes abdominal tenderness; rarely shock, ocular problems	Sudden onset of fever, headache, backache, vomiting, marked prostration, and delirium; small blisters form crusts which fall off 10 d to 40 d after first lesions appear; opportunistic infection	Sudden illness with malaise, spiking fevers, rigors, severe headache, photophobia, and myalgias
Treatment	No specific treatment exists. Severe cases require intensive supportive care, as patients are frequently dehydrated and in need of intravenous fluids.	No specific therapy; supportive therapy essential	No studies, but IV ribavirin (30 mg/kg/6 h for 4 d, then 7.5 mg/kg/8 h for 6 d) should be effective	Vaccinia immune globulin (VIG) and supportive therapy	Supportive treatments only
Potential as Biological Agent	High—actually weaponized by former Soviet Union biological program	Unknown	Difficulties with mosquitos as vectors	Possible, especially since routine smallpox vaccination programs have been eliminated world-wide (part of USSR offense bioprogram)	High—former U.S. and U.S.S.R. offensive biological programs weaponized both liquid and dry forms for aerosol distribution

Table 2–2. Viral agents–Continued

Biological Agent/Disease	Yellow Fever Virus	Dengue Fever Virus	Ebola Virus	Congo-Crimean Hemorrhagic Fever Virus
Likely Method of Dissemination	Mosquito-borne	Mosquito-borne	1. Direct contact 2. Aerosol (BA)	Unknown
Transmissible Person to Person	No	No	Moderate	Yes
Incubation Period	3 d to 6 d	3 d to 15 d	4 d to 16 d	7 d to 12 d
Duration of Illness	2 wk	1 wk	Death between 7 d to 16 d	9 d to 12 d
Lethality	10 % to 20 % death in severe cases or full recovery after 2 d to 3 d	5 % average case fatality by producing shock and hemorrhage, leading to death	High for Zaire strain; moderate with Sudan	15 % to 20 %
Vaccine Efficacy (for aerosol exposure)/ Antitoxin	Vaccine available; confers immunity for >10 yr	Vaccine available	No vaccine	No vaccine available; prophylactic ribavirin may be effective
Symptoms and Effects	Sudden onset of chills, fever, prostration, aches, muscular pain, congestion, severe gastrointestinal disturbances, liver damage and jaundice; hemorrhage from skin and gums	Sudden onset of fever, chills, intense headache, pain behind eyes, joint and muscle pain, exhaustion and prostration	Mild febrile illness, then vomiting, diarrhea, rash, kidney and liver failure, internal and external hemorrhage (begins 5th day), and petechiae	Fever, easy bleeding, petechiae, hypotension and shock; flushing of face and chest, edema, vomiting, diarrhea
Treatment	No specific treatment; supportive treatment (bed rest and fluids) for even the mildest cases	No specific therapy; supportive therapy essential	No specific therapy; supportive therapy essential	No specific treatment
Potential as Biological Agent	High, if efficient dissemination device is employed	Unknown	Former Soviet Union	Unknown

10

Table 2–3. Rickettsiae

Biological Agent/Disease	Endemic Typhus	Epidemic Typhus	Q Fever	Rocky Mountain Spotted Fever
Likely Method of Dissemination	1. Contaminated feces 2. Infected insect larvae 3. Rat or flea bites	1. Contaminated feces 2. Infected insect larvae	1. Sabotage (food supply) 2. Aerosol	Infected wood ticks
Transmissible Person to Person	No	No	Rare	No
Incubation Period	6 d to 14 d	6 d to 15 d	14 d to 26 d	3 d to 14 d
Duration of Illness	Unknown	Unknown	Weeks	Unknown
Lethality	1 %, increasing in people >50 yr old	10 % to 40 % untreated; increases with age	Very low	15 % to 20 % untreated (higher in adults); treated—death rare with specific therapy (tetracycline or chloramphenicol)
Vaccine Efficacy (for aerosol exposure)/ Antitoxin	Unknown	Vaccine confers protection of uncertain duration	94 % protection against 3500 LD_{50}s in guinea pigs	No vaccine
Symptoms and Effects	Sudden onset of headache, chills, prostration, fever, pain; maculae eruption on 5th day to 6th day on upper body, spreading to all but palms, soles, or face, but milder than epidemic form	Sudden onset of headache, chills, prostration, fever, pain; maculae eruption on 5th day to 6th day on upper body, spreading to all but palms, soles, or face	Mild symptoms (chills, headaches, fever, chest pains, perspiration, loss of appetite)	Fever and joint pain, muscular pain; skin rash that spreads rapidly from ankles and wrists to legs, arms, and chest; aversion to light
Treatment	Antibiotics (tetracycline and chloramphenicol); supportive treatment and prevention of secondary infections	Antibiotics (tetracycline and chloramphenicol); supportive treatment and prevention of secondary infections	Tetracycline (500 mg/ 6 h, 5 d to 7 d) or doxycycline (100 mg/ 12 h, 5 d to 7 d) also, combined Erthyromycin (500 mg/6 h) and rifampin (600 mg/d)	Antibiotics— tetracycline or chloramphenicol
Potential as Biological Agent	Uncertain—broad range of incubation (6 d to 14 d) period could cause infection of force deploying biological agent	Uncertain—broad range of incubation (6 d to 14 d) period could cause infection of force deploying biological agent	Highly infectious, is delivered in aerosol form. Dried agent is very stable; stable in aerosol form.	Unknown

11

Table 2–4. Biological toxins

Biological Agent/Disease	Botulinum Toxin	Staphylococcal enterotoxin B	Tricothecene mycotoxins	Ricin (Isolated from Castor Beans)	Saxitoxin
Likely Method of Dissemination	1. Aerosol 2. Sabotage (food and water)	1. Sabotage (food supply) 2. Aerosol	1. Aerosol 2. Sabotage	1. Aerosol 2. Sabotage (food & water)	Contaminated shellfish; in biological scenario, inhalation or toxic projectile
Transmissible Person to Person	No	No	No	No	No
Incubation Period	Variable (hours to days)	3 h to 12 h	2 h to 4 h	Hours to days	5 min to 1 h
Duration of Illness	Death in 24 h to 72 h; lasts months if not lethal	Hours	Days to months	Days—death within 10 d to 12 d for ingestion	Death in 2 h to 12 h
Lethality	5 % to 60 %, untreated <5 % treated	<1 %	Moderate	100 %, without treatment	High without respiratory support
Vaccine Efficacy (for aerosol exposure)/ Antitoxin	Botulism antitoxin (IND) Prophylaxis toxoid (IND) Toxolide	No vaccine	No vaccine	No vaccine	No vaccine
Symptoms and Effects	Ptosis; weakness, dizziness, dry mouth and throat, blurred vision and diplopia, flaccid paralysis	Sudden chills, fever, headache, myalgia, nonproductive cough, nausea, vomiting and diarrhea	Skin—pain, pruritis, redness and vesicles, sloughing of epidermis; respiratory—nose and throat pain, discharge, sneezing, coughing, chest pain, hemoptysis	Weakness, fever, cough, pulmonary edema, severe respiratory distress	Light headedness, tingling of extremities, visual disturbances, memory loss, respiratory distress, death
Treatment	Antitoxin with respiratory support (ventilation)	Pain relievers and cough suppressants for mild cases; for severe cases, may need mechanical breathing and fluid replenishment	No specific antidote or therapeutic regimen is available; supportive and symptomatic care	Oxygen, plus drugs to reduce inflammation and support cardiac and circulatory functions; if ingested, empty the stomach and intestines; replace lost fluids	Induce vomiting, provide respiratory care, including artificial respiration
Potential as Biological Agent	Not very toxic via aerosol route; extremely lethal if delivered orally. Since covert poisoning is indistinguishable from natural botulism, poisoning could have limited use	Moderate—could be used in food and limited amounts of water (for example, at salad bars); LD_{50} is sufficiently small to prevent detection	High—used in aerosol form ("yellow rain") in Laos, Kampuchea and Afghanistan (through 1981)	Has been used in 1978—Markov murder (see app. A, ref. 6); included on prohibited Schedule I chemicals list for Chemical Weapons Convention; high potential for use in aerosol form	Moderate, aerosol form is highly toxic

3. CHALLENGES TO BIOLOGICAL AGENT DETECTION

Biological agents are effective in very low doses. Therefore, biological agent detection systems need to exhibit high **sensitivity** (i.e., be able to *detect* very small amounts of biological agents). The complex and rapidly changing environmental background also requires these detection systems to exhibit a high degree of **selectivity** (i.e., be able to *discriminate* biological agents from other harmless biological and nonbiological material present in the environment). A third challenge that needs to be addressed is **speed** or **response**. These combined requirements provide a significant technical challenge. Additionally, there has been limited development in the area of biological agent detection equipment in the commercial market (i.e., hand-held devices). There are several detection systems being developed and tested by the military that show promise. However, these systems are relatively complicated, require training for successful operation and maintenance, and are expensive to purchase and operate. It is expected that over the course of the next 5 years, commercial instrumentation, hardened for use in the field, may become available at reasonable costs.

The purpose of this section is to identify some of the major challenges associated with biological agent detection. Specifically, section 3.1 addresses challenges associated with the ambient environment, section 3.2 discusses challenges with selectivity, section 3.3 discusses challenges with sensitivity, and section 3.4 addresses challenges with sampling.

3.1 The Ambient Environment

The environment in which we live and operate is an extremely complex and dynamic medium. The meteorological, physical, chemical, and biological constituents of a "normal" atmospheric environment all impact our ability to detect biological agents. In order to understand the complex effect that the ambient environment can have on biological agent detection, the remainder of this section discusses specifics of the particulate background, the biological background, and the optical background, respectively.

3.1.1 The Particulate Background

Particulates in the atmosphere originate from a number of sources. Dust, dirt, pollen, and fog are all examples of naturally occurring particulates found in the air. Man-made particulates such as engine exhaust, smoke, and industrial effluents (smokestacks) also contribute significantly to the environmental particulate background. Therefore, the particulate background can be defined as the combination of natural and man-made particles in the atmosphere that are nonpathogenic (does not cause disease) in nature. Biological agents (not including toxins) consist of particulates of pathogenic (disease causing) cells. The particulate background can change on a minute-by-minute basis depending on the meteorological conditions at the time. For example, the particulate background next to a road will change dramatically depending on whether there is traffic on the road disturbing the dust, or if the road is empty. Likewise, if there is little wind, not many particulates are carried into the atmosphere; however, when the wind begins to blow, it can carry many particulates from the immediate vicinity, as well as from remote locations. The challenge for a biological detection system is to be able to discriminate between all of the naturally occurring particulates and the biological agent particulates.

Particle counters can be used to monitor changes in the particulate background on a real-time basis because these systems see particles in the air and can count them. If the number of particles increases rapidly, it is possible that biological agents are being used; however, **it must be stressed that particle counters cannot determine if the particulates are dust, pollen, engine exhaust, or biological agents**. Other, more sensitive and selective, tests must be performed on the particulates to determine if biological agents are present. Particle counters are best used in a detection system where the particle counter activates a sampler that collects a sample of the particles for a more detailed analysis.

3.1.2 The Biological Background

Our environment is filled with living creatures that form a large and complex biological background from which we must identify biological agents. The challenge for a biological agent detection system is to be able to pick out a specific signal from the biological agent while rejecting, or at best minimizing, any signals originating from the nonpathogenic (nontoxic) biological background. This is a significant challenge given the amount of biological particulates in the environment. Research has identified a variety of potential bio-aerosol sources (i.e., adjoining crop fields that are fertilized with "night soil," garbage incinerators, landfills, industrial areas, and dairy farms). Studies have shown that the concentration of bio-aerosols depends on the location of the measurement. In Oregon, a study showed that the concentration of bio-aerosol in an urban setting was six times greater than along the coast and almost three times greater than in a rural setting.

Data shown in figure 3–1 suggest that not only do biological aerosols vary by location, they also vary significantly by time of day.

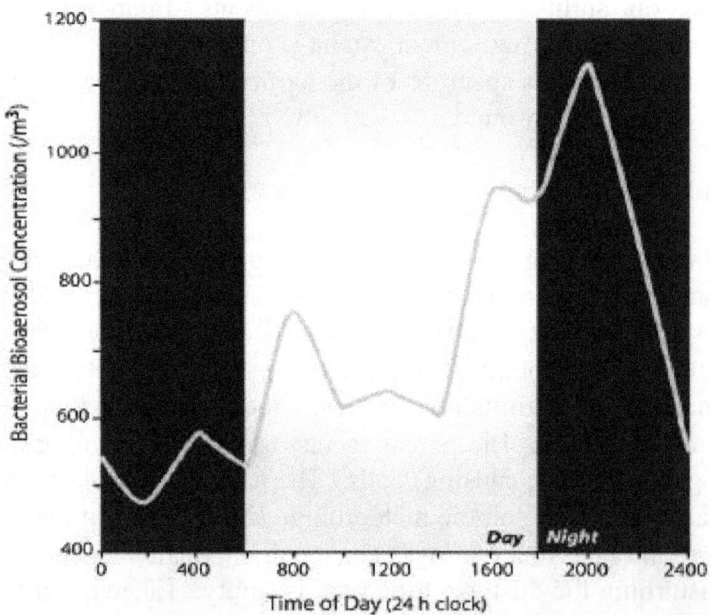

Figure 3–1. Airborne bacterial concentration fluctuation in a single day[4]

[4] Aerosolized bacterial concentration fluctuation over a 24 h period. The vertical (y) axis is bacterial concentration per cubic meter of air. The horizontal (x) axis is the time of day; shaded regions represent nighttime hours, and the clear region is daytime hours. The graph shows that in the early morning hours, the airborne bacterial concentration is low, but it increases rapidly during daylight, reaching a maximum at 8:00 a.m. It then falls to a lower level for most of the day and significantly increases towards the end of the day.

3.1.3 The Optical Background

Systems such as laser or passive infrared (IR) systems rely on optical properties for detection of biological agents. They can be affected by micron range particulates, as well as by other obstructions to visibility such as rain, fog, snow, and dust. Aerosols and precipitation may act like mirrors, reflecting and diffusing the light energy to and from the detector, and in the case of some aerosols, return false signatures (e.g., fluorescence from engine exhaust and pollens may confuse some ultraviolet (UV) based systems). Consequently, different standoff systems are affected to different degrees by precipitation and aerosols. Infrared-based systems, as a rule, tend to be less affected by atmospheric clarity than UV-based systems.

3.2 Selectivity of the Detection System

Detection systems must exhibit a high degree of selectivity for biological agents. The selectivity of a detection system can be defined as its ability to discriminate between the target agent and the environmental interferants. The degree to which the selectivity of a system is affected by interferants depends on the type of measurement being conducted. For example, dust and pollen can be considered interferants for a particle counter, while water vapor and fog are interferants for standoff IR detection systems. For biological agent monitoring, the most difficult interferants originate from the biological background (i.e., live nonpathogenic matter). Generally, the more selective systems require more sample processing and multiple detectors. A single system for detection of biological agents in the environment that exhibits high selectivity currently does not exist as a commercially available item. The selective systems currently developed by the military are limited to detection of a small number of agents and are prohibitively expensive.

3.3 Sensitivity

Detection systems must exhibit high sensitivity for the biological agents because of the agent's low effective doses (fig. 1). Sensitivity can be defined as the smallest amount of target agent that gives a reproducible response above the system noise for a detector. The system noise can be defined as the random fluctuation of the detector response and is generally associated with small variations in electronic output. Other noise that degrades the sensitivity is caused by interferants in the environment. In a perfect detection system, the system sensitivity (only dependent on the electronic noise) defines how much of the target agent can be detected. Interferants cause the sensitivity to decrease because the system needs more of the target agent to distinguish it from the interferants.

3.4 Sampling

The primary infection route from exposure to biological agents is through inhalation, and it is likely that most of the initial aerosol would have settled by the time emergency first responders arrive on the scene of an incident. This does not lessen the possibility of infection of the first responders by reaersolization of the agent but requires that the emergency first responders take more than just air samples for analysis. It may be critical for the emergency first responders to conduct environmental (soil/water) sampling and air and swipe tests to corroborate the occurrence of a biological attack and to determine if the biological agent is still present.

Emergency first responders may only be involved in post-incident activities and may not have any need for early warning capabilities.

Since sampling is a key issue for all analytical devices, the way a sample is taken and how it is handled will affect the outcome of the analysis. In a point collection/detection scenario, sampling for biological agent particlates in the air is especially difficult due to the low effective doses of these agents. To sample biological agents effectively, samplers are used that pass large volumes of air through the sampler, dispersing the small amount of agent contained in a large volume of air into a small volume of water, thereby forming a concentrated mixture of particulates in water. By concentrating the biological particulates, current detection systems that are not able to detect biological agents at low dose levels can detect the biological agents in the concentrated mixture.

4. BIOLOGICAL DETECTION SYSTEM COMPONENTS

The effective detection of biological agents in the environment requires a multicomponent analysis system because of the complexity of the environment. Other variables contributing to the effectiveness of detection of biological agents are the detection process itself and the efficient use of consumables in the field. Biological agent detection systems generally consist of four components: the trigger/cue, the collector, the detector, and the identifier. Figure 4–1 shows a flow diagram for a typical point detection automated architecture system. The function of these components is described in the remainder of this section, while section 5 will provide representative examples of each component.

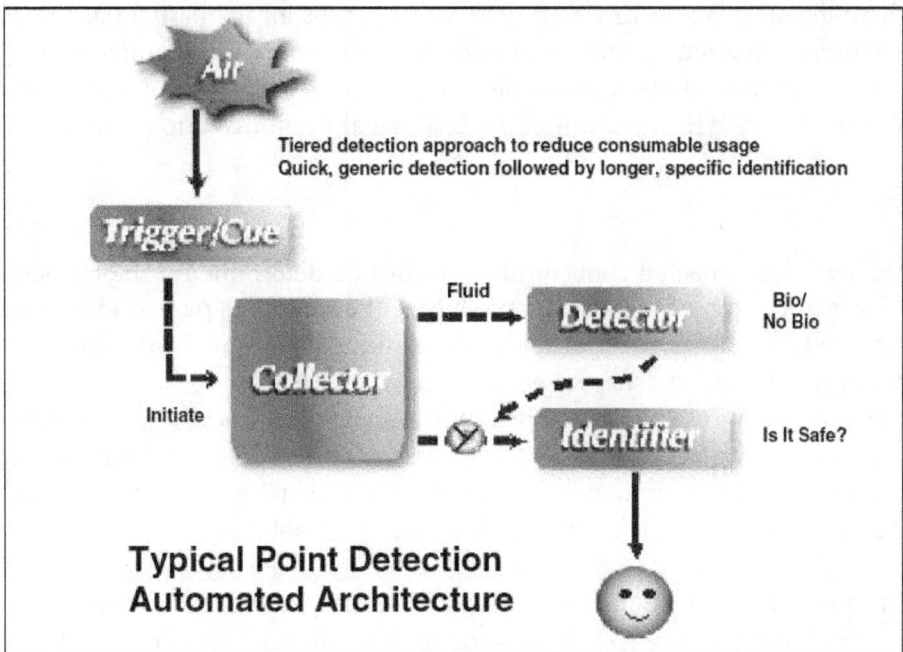

**Figure 4–1. Typical point detection automated architecture
(with a combined trigger/cue)**

4.1 Trigger/Cue

Trigger technology is the first level of detection that determines any change in the particulate background at the sensor, indicating a possible introduction of biological agents. Detection of an increase in the particulate concentration by the trigger causes the remaining components of the detection system to begin operation. The trigger function typically provides a means of continuously monitoring the air without unnecessary use of consumables, thus keeping the logistical burden of biological agent detection low.

To reduce false positives (alarm with no biological agent) and false negatives (no alarm with agent), many detection systems combine trigger technology with a second detector technology (such as fluorescence that provides more selectivity) into a single technology known as cueing. Most effective cueing technologies can detect airborne particulates in near real time and can discriminate between biological agent aerosol particles and other particles in air, avoiding unnecessary system activation. For example, a cueing device monitors the air for particulates as does any other trigger device. When the particulate concentration increases, the cue determines if the particulates are biological in nature. The cue device generally uses a fluorescence detector to make this determination. If the particulates are found to be biological, the cue device activates the collector for sample collection.

4.2 Collector

As discussed in section 3.4, sampling of the biological agent is a crucial part of the identification system. The effective dose for some agents is extremely small; therefore, highly efficient collection devices must be employed. One type of collector pumps large volumes of air through a chamber where the air mixes with water. The water scrubs all the particulates from the air, resulting in a sample containing particulates suspended in water. Once collected in the water, the sample is further concentrated by evaporation of a portion of the water. After concentration, the sample moves into the analytical section of the biological agent detection system.

4.3 Detector

Once a sample has been collected/concentrated, it must be determined if the particulates are biological or inorganic in origin. To accomplish this, the sample is passed to a generic detection component that analyzes the aerosol particles to determine if they are biological in origin. This component may also classify the suspect aerosol by broad category (e.g., spore, bacterium, toxin/macromolecule, or virus). In its simplest form, the detector acts as a "gateway" for further analysis. If the sample exhibits characteristics of biological particles, it is passed through to the next level of analysis. If the sample does not exhibit such characteristics, it is not passed to the next level of analysis, thereby conserving analytical consumables.

It is important to note that detection has traditionally taken place after the trigger function. For example, an aerosol particle sizer (APS) triggers, then a detector (e.g., flow cytometer) examines the aerosol for biological content. Many of the newer detection technologies combine the trigger and detection functionalities into a single instrument, creating a cueing instrument. As described in section 4.1, the cue first detects a rise in particulates then determines if the particulates are of biological origin. If the sample is biological, the collector gathers a sample and passes it directly to the identifier.

4.4 Identifier

An identifier is a device that specifically identifies the type of biological agent collected by the system. Identifiers are generally limited to a preselected set of agents and cannot identify agents outside of this set without the addition of new identifier chemistry/equipment or preprogramming. Because the identifier performs the final and highest level of agent detection, it is the most critical component of the detection architecture and has the widest variety of technologies and equipment available. The information obtained from the identifier is then used to determine protection requirements and treatment of exposed personnel.

5. OVERVIEW OF BIOLOGICAL AGENT DETECTION SYSTEM TECHNOLOGIES

The applicability of biological agent detection equipment to emergency first responders will depend on the characteristics of the detection equipment, the type of biological agent to be detected, and the objective of the emergency first responder unit. Good analytical results from the various analyzers will depend on the ability to effectively sample the environment and deliver the biological agent to the analyzer.

Biological detection systems are currently in the research and early development stages. There are some commercially available devices that have limited utility (responding only to a small number of agents) and are generally high cost items. Because commercially available biological warfare (BW) detection systems and/or components exhibit limited utility in detecting and identifying BW agents and are also costly, it is strongly recommended that first responders be very careful when considering a purchase of any device that claims to detect BW agents. This is a very different situation when compared to chemical detection equipment; there are various technologies for detection of chemical agents and toxic industrial materials (TIMs) that can be purchased by the emergency first responder. One reason for the lack of available biological detection equipment is that detection of biological agents requires extremely high sensitivity (because of the very low effective dose needed to cause infection and spread the disease) and an unusually high degree of selectivity (because of the large and diverse biological background in the environment).

Another reason for the lack of biological detection equipment is that biological agents, compared to chemical agents, are very complex systems of molecules, which makes them much more difficult to identify. For example, Ionization/Ion Mobility Spectrometry (IMS), an excellent (though expensive) system for collection, detection, and identification of chemical agents, cannot detect or discriminate biological agents in its present form. In fact, the need for high-efficiency collection and concentration of the sample, high sensitivities, and high selectivities make all chemical detectors in their current form unusable for biological agent detection.

Because of the need for high selectivity and sensitivity, the biological detection systems are necessarily complex devices consisting of various subunits. Each subunit performs a specific collection, detection, and identification task. In this section, the various units and subunits that make up biological agent point and standoff detection systems are described. Specifically, section 5.1 discusses the separate technologies utilized with point detection, section 5.2 discusses standoff technologies (both short range and long range), and section 5.3 addresses passive standoff detection.

For reference only, examples of the size and complexity of integrated biological detection systems are presented in figure 5-1 and figure 5-2. They are the Biological Integrated Detection Systems (BIDS) from the United States and a cutaway picture of the Integrated Biological Integrated Detection System from the United Kingdom, respectively.

*Figure 5–1. Biological Integrated
Detection System (BIDS)*

*Figure 5–2. Cutaway of the UK Integrated
Biological Detection System (IBDS)*

5.1 Point Detection Technologies

Point detectors are those sensors that must be in the aerosol plume or have the suspect biological agent introduced into/onto them for sensing. Point detection systems have traditionally encompassed the following components: trigger/cue (nonspecific biological agent detectors), sampler/collector, and identifier (specific identification technologies).

5.1.1 Trigger/Cue (Nonspecific Biological Agent Detectors)

The function of the trigger is to provide early warning that a change in the background air has occurred. Operation of a trigger requires establishing background aerosol levels in a specific location and then sensing that an increase in the aerosol particle count in the background has occurred. A trigger is nonselective and does not identify the organism but only indicates a change in the background aerosol level. Since a trigger is nonselective, a detector is required if there is no cue.

A cueing device is first able to determine when there is an increase in particulates and then is able to distinguish between concentrations of biological aerosols and nonbiological aerosols (nonspecific biological agent detection). Descriptions of several detector technologies are presented in section 5.1.3.

Brief descriptions of trigger/cue technologies are presented in the section below.

5.1.1.1 Particle Measurement

One technique used for nonspecific detection is counting the relative number of particles in specific size ranges (typically 0.5 μm to 30 μm). A variety of technologies are used for particle monitoring and/or counting, but aerodynamic particle sizing has been directly applied to field biological agent detection. Several examples of particle measurement technologies follow.

Aerodynamic Particle Sizing (APS): The particle-laden air stream is drawn into the APS device through a flow nozzle, producing a controlled high-speed aerosol jet. During the measurement period, the air velocity remains constant but because of the different sizes of the individual particles within the jet, they accelerate at different rates based on their relative sizes (smaller particles accelerate faster than larger particles). A laser beam measures the time of flight of the individual particles.

High Volume Aerodynamic Particle Sizer (HVAPS): The HVAPS passes an accelerated, concentrated air stream past a laser-based particle counter to obtain aerosol particle size distribution and concentration. This instrument cannot discriminate biological from non-biological aerosols.

Met-One: The Met-One is a compact, low-power aerosol particle sizer and counter about the size of a large, hand-held calculator. This device is available commercially and is typically used to monitor clean rooms. The Met-One draws an air sample through a laser-illuminated sample volume where airborne particles scatter light. The light scattered by individual particles is then detected using a photodiode. Like the HVAPS, the Met-One looks for a statistically significant rise in aerosol concentration over background; however, the Met-One is not able to resolve the particle sizes as finely as the HVAPS. The Met-One gains its size and weight savings through a combination of low airflow and use of a low-power, diode laser.

5.1.1.2 Fluorescence Methods

Fluorescence approaches involve excitation of molecular components of a material with light, usually in the ultra violet (UV) region of the spectrum. The excited component spontaneously reverts to an unexcited state followed by emission of light at different wavelengths. Because the emission spectrum is specific to the molecular component being irradiated and the excitation wavelength, this phenomenon can be exploited in detection of biological material (biofluorescence). Biofluorescence-based techniques generate data from only some specific molecular components of biological material, allowing it to be a tool for nonspecific agent detection by providing the emission spectrum of a common material (i.e., tryptophan) when an unknown sample is irradiated.

The two types of fluorescence measurement approaches are primary and secondary. In primary biofluorescence, some common, naturally fluorescent component of biomaterials, such as tryptophan (an amino acid building block of protein), is measured. Secondary fluorescence methods involve introducing (tagging) a special fluorophore (i.e., fluorochrome stain) to the sample before UV irradiation. Secondary methods require a longer measurement time and add complexity to the measurement process. Several devices that use biofluorescence technologies are included in the remainder of this section.

Fluorescent Aerodynamic Particle Sizer (FLAPS): FLAPS is an Aerodynamic Particle Sizer (APS) that has been modified to include an additional laser (blue or UV wavelength) that provides for aerosol particle fluorescence in addition to standard particle size information. Besides obtaining the aerodynamic particle size, the laser's signal acts as a trigger to open a time window in which to look for particle fluorescence. The information obtained from this technology will be more specific than the current standard particle size and number density results.

The FLAPS II device is part of the Canadian Integrated Biological Agent Detection System (CIBADS), a.k.a., the 4WARN detection suite. The CIBADS is an integrated system of components developed by the Canadian Ministry of Defense that currently contains a detector/trigger function, sample collection function, meteorological instrumentation, and communications equipment. A picture of the FLAPS II is presented in figure 5–3, and the 4WARN system from Canada is presented in figure 5–4.

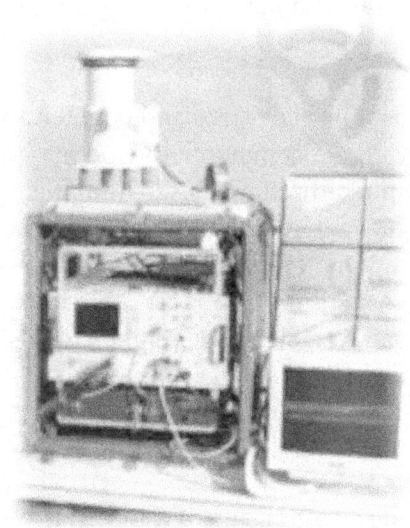

Figure 5–3. FLAPS II (component of the Canadian 4WARN System)

Figure 5–4. Canadian Integrated Biological-Chemical Agent Detection System (CIBADS)/4WARN

A variation of the FLAPS particle sizer is the Ultra Violet Aerodynamic Particle Sizer (UVAPS) that uses time-of-flight particle sizing, light scattering, and UV fluorescence intensity to nonspecifically detect biological agents in air samples. The UVAPS (as well as the FLAPS) is commercially available from TSI Inc., Particle Instruments.

The Biological Aerosol Warning System (BAWS) is effective as a trigger/cue technology. The BAWS uses a micro-laser-based system that analyzes two biological fluorescence wavelengths to determine if an unusual biological event is happening. The BAWS does not count aerosol particles. It can detect in real time and can discriminate biological agent aerosol particles from other particles in the air to avoid false triggers.

A technique called Portable Biofluorosensor (PBS) was used during Operation Desert Storm. The technique used UV light from a xenon flash lamp to excite airborne aerosols and aerosols dissolved in water. The excitation wavelength minimized interference from dust, exhaust, etc., but did not eliminate false positives. Liquid samples containing spores provided better analysis results than airborne samples.

The Single-Particle Fluorescence Counter (SPFC), developed by the Naval Research Laboratory (NRL), employs continuous airflow across a 780 nm laser-diode beam, resulting in light scattering from individual aerosol particles in the air. The total intensity of scattered light is measured, and particle size is calculated. This event also triggers a 266 nm UV laser pulse that causes fluorescent particles to emit light at a different wavelength (i.e., the particles fluoresce).

5.1.2 Samplers/Collectors

Since an extremely low airborne concentration of biological agents can be difficult to detect but still cause severe effects, a device to concentrate particles/aerosols in the air stream is needed. A collector/concentrator samples the atmosphere and concentrates the airborne particles into a liquid medium for analysis. Several types of samplers/collectors have been evaluated for biological agent detection. The principal differences between collection for biological agent detection and other types of aerosol or particulate sampling are (1) biological agent sampling is normally targeted at living organisms, so the sampling techniques must preserve and not harm the collected sample; (2) most biological detection and identification technologies require a liquid sample, so the collection must be from an aerosol or particulate in a liquid; and (3) the liquid sample must be highly concentrated and available for rapid analysis since response time is critical.

A collector is most useful when it is part of a detection system. When the collector receives a signal from a trigger indicating a change in the background level, an air sample is collected, and airborne particles are concentrated into a liquid medium.

The efficiency of a collector at capturing and concentrating aerosol samples typically affects several downstream functions. In virtually all systems, the collectors feed into the identification component of the biological detection system and also provide the samples that are used for confirmatory identification and forensic analysis.

Collectors can be broadly divided into two groups. One group contains collectors that are large and consume much power. These collectors, on the whole, have a high collection and concentration efficiency and are candidates for detection systems that operate well away from the line or point of agent release. The other group contains those collectors that consume little power, are hand-portable, and have relatively low collection and concentration efficiencies. Whereas these collectors would work well in high agent concentrations (e.g., near the point or line of release, or perhaps indoors), they would fail to provide an adequate sample to downstream instruments. It should also be noted that collectors significantly contribute to the overall weight, size, and power requirements of a detection system.

Examples of sampler/collector technologies include Viable Particle Size Samplers (Impactors), Virtual Impactors, Cyclones, and Bubblers/Impingers.

5.1.2.1 Viable Particle Size Samplers (Impactors)

A conventional impactor operates by accelerating an air stream of particles through a nozzle and diverting the air stream against an impaction plate maintained at a fixed distance from the nozzle. The larger particles are unable to follow the fluid streamlines (air in this case) because of their large inertia; smaller particles follow the fluid streamlines and exit the sampler.

The impactor usually has multiple stages and each stage contains a number of precision-drilled orifices that are a constant size for each stage. Particle laden air enters the instrument, and the airborne particles are directed towards the collection surfaces by the jet orifices. Any particle not collected by a specific stage follows the stream of air around the edge of the collection surface to the next stage. The collection plate is typically a petri dish with selective agar (selective to a specific organism). The plates are incubated (typically 24 h to 48 h) and after incubation, the number of colonies on each plate are counted.

5.1.2.2 Virtual Impactors

A virtual impactor is similar to a conventional impactor but uses a different impaction surface. The flat plate of the conventional impactor is replaced by a collection probe, and the larger particles penetrate the collection probe instead of striking a flat plate. By properly controlling the airflow in the impactor, it is possible to collect particles in a specific size range. In addition, the final stage can then aim the particle stream onto a liquid, resulting in a highly concentrated liquid sample.

The Liquid Sampler (PEM-0020) with carousel is manufactured by Power Engineering and Manufacturing, Inc. The device uses virtual impaction to collect and concentrate airborne particles onto liquid film. The operator can select the number of samples to be collected (up to 10) and can choose from several preprogrammed sampling protocols that vary the volume and the collection time for each tube. Initiation of the sample collection is by external trigger or manual push button. The unit automatically repositions the carousel at the end of the collection cycle. The entire carousel can be quickly removed and replaced.

The BioVIC™ Aerosol Collector, developed by MesoSystems Technology, Inc., serves as a front-end air sampler for biological detection systems. It is an impacter that preconcentrates the air stream, capturing large numbers of particles either into a small volume of liquid, into a small air stream, or onto a solid surface for delivery into the sensor. The BioVIC™ can be used with PCR, fluorescent-based optical sensors, mass spectrometry, pyrolysis GC mass spectrometry, or flow cytometry. Figure 5–5 shows a picture of the BioVIC™ Aerosol Collector.

Figure 5–5. BioVIC™ Aerosol Collector, MesoSystems Technology, Inc.

5.1.2.3 Cyclone Samplers

A cyclone is an inertial device that is commonly used in industrial applications for removing particles from large airflows. A particle-laden air stream enters the cyclone body and forms an outer spiral moving downward towards the bottom of the cyclone. The larger particles are collected on the outer wall due to centrifugal force, and the smaller particles follow the airstream that forms the inner spiral and leave through the exit tube. Water spray applied to the outer walls of a cyclone facilitate particle collection and preservation. Several examples of cyclone samplers are discussed in the remainder of this section.

The Interim Biological Agent Detector System (IBADS) was initially developed for the Navy. It uses a wetted-wall cyclone to collect the aerosol particles into an aqueous sample. Variants of this device are in use in the Portal Shield Biological Detection System and in the current version of the Joint Biological Point Detection System (JBPDS). See figure 5–6 for an example of the JBPDS.

The Smart Air Sampler System (SASS 2000) is a device that has been independently developed by Research International and also uses wetted-wall cyclone technology. This hand-held device can operate on battery power. An example of the SASS 2000 is shown in Figure 5–7.

Figure 5–6. Joint Biological Point Detection System (JBPDS)

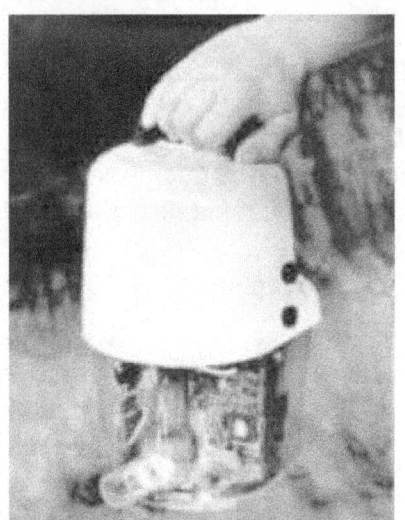

Figure 5–7. Smart Air Sampler System (SASS 2000), Research International

The Portable High-Throughput Liquid Aerosol Air Sampler System (PHTLAAS) is a small hand-held device that uses technology similar to the wetted-wall cyclone technology. This instrument concentrates the contaminants found in a large volume of air into a small volume of liquid for ultrasensitive semiquantitative detection. Zaromb Research Corporation has independently developed this device.

5.1.2.4 Hand-Held Sampling Kit

The Department of Defense Biological Sampling Kit (DoD BSK) is a prepackaged kit containing a panel of eight hand-held immunochromatographic assay (HHA) devices (i.e., able to simultaneously identify up to eight different biological agents), a dropper bottle of buffer solution, two sterile cotton-tipped swabs, and an instruction card. The DoD BSK is included in the sampler/collection section because it is used for field screening where the concentration of agent is expected to be high and not for positive identification. The kit is not to be used for screening soil samples since some soil constituents can cross-react with the HHA reagents if present in high enough concentrations. In addition, the DoD BSK should not be used for screening heavily dust-laden surfaces. Also, the kit is not sensitive enough to detect the minute amounts of precipitate that may fall out from an attack that originated from a distant location (e.g., a long line source release from several kilometers away).

The advantages of the DoD BSK are that it is inexpensive, reliable, easy to use, and the assays in the kit are improved concurrent with the assays in the other detection programs. Disadvantages of the DoD BSK are that it does not possess a generic detection capability (it is an identifier), and each kit is for one time use only.

5.1.2.5 Hand-Held Sampling Device

The BioCapture™ BT-500 Air Sampler was developed by MesoSystems Technology, Inc., and incorporates the BioVIC™ Aerosol Collector, also developed by MesoSystems Technology, Inc. It is a hand-held, battery-powered air sampler that collects airborne samples for quantifying concentration levels. The microbes are captured and concentrated into an aqueous sample for analysis by whole cell rapid detection, nucleic acid, or other liquid-based sensor systems. The removable single-use cartridge can also be archived for evidence of a biological incident. An example of the BioCapture™ BT-500 Air Sampler is shown in figure 5–8.

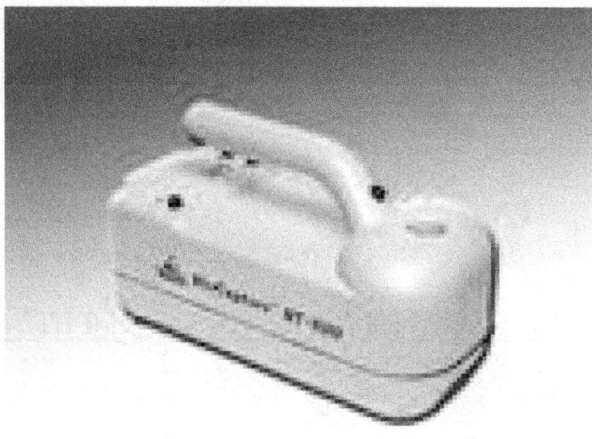

Figure 5–8. BioCapture™ BT-500 Air Sampler, MesoSystems Technology, Inc.

5.1.3 Detectors

Detectors are those components/instruments used to determine if the particulates are biological or inorganic in origin and if further analysis of the sample is needed. Some detectors require additional processing of a sample before it can be introduced into the detector, while others can use a sample directly from the environment. In this section, detectors are broadly divided into two groups, wet detection (flow cytometry) and dry detection (mass spectrometry).

5.1.3.1 Wet Detection (Flow Cytometry)

Cytometry is the measurement of both physical and chemical characteristics of cells. Flow cytometry (widely used as a wet detector for biological agents) uses the same technique as cytometry but makes the measurements of cells or other particles present in a moving fluid stream as they pass through a testing point. It measures particle sizes and counts particles in liquid suspensions through the use of laser light scattering. Flow cytometers involve sophisticated fluidics, laser optics, electronic detectors, analog to digital converters, and computers to provide an automated method for bio-chemical analysis and to process thousands of cells in a few seconds. Typically, the sample will also be treated by addition of a fluorescent dye that reacts with biological material (e.g., DNA). Flow cytometers have been commercially available since the early 1970s and increasingly have been used since then. Examples utilizing this technology are the Los Alamos National Laboratory Flow Cytometer (LANL) and the Becton Dickenson Flow Cytometer (FACSCaliber). They will be briefly discussed below.

The Los Alamos National Laboratory (LANL) Flow Cytometer employs a green (HeNe) laser diode. Particle size is measured by two light-scatter detectors, and fluorescence is measured by two photomultiplier tubes. This instrument is also known as the "Mini-Flow Cytometer" and is just 1.15 ft^3 in size, 30 lb in weight, and requires 1 kW of power.

The B-D Flow Cytometer FACSCount, manufactured by Becton Dickenson, employs a direct two-color immunogluorescence method and uses a green (HeNe) laser.

The B-D Flow Cytometer FACSCaliber, manufactured by Becton Dickenson, is a four-color Modular Analytical Flow Cytometer that uses a 15 mW air-cooled blue argon-ion laser and a red laser diode. The FACSCalibur also has an optional sorter. Figure 5–9 shows an example of the B-D Flow Cytometer FACSCaliber.

Figure 5–9. B–D Flow Cytometer FACSCaliber, Becton Dickenson

5.1.3.2 Dry Detectors (Mass Spectrometry)

Mass spectrometry (MS) is a microanalytical technique that requires only a few nanograms of analyte to obtain characteristic information on the structure and molecular weight of the analyte. The technique ionizes molecules and breaks them apart into characteristic fragments (the fragmentation pattern constitutes its "mass spectrum"). The mass spectrometer requires that samples be introduced in the gaseous state. Sample introduction into the mass spectrometer can be by direct air/gas sampling, a direct insertion probe, membrane inlets, effluent from a gas chromatograph (GC), effluent from a high-performance liquid chromatograph (HPLC), capillary electrophoresis, and effluent from pyrolysis devices. Several examples of detection equipment utilizing mass spectrometry are discussed below.

The <u>Pyrolysis-Gas Chromatography-Ion Mobility Spectrometer (PY-GC-IMS)</u> combusts, or pyrolyzes, the biological particles. The biological pyrolysis products are then separated using gas chromatography. Once separated, the individual pyrolysis products are introduced into an ion mobility spectrometer for analysis. This technology is still quite new and was developed in a collaborative effort between Edgewood Chemical Biological Center (ECBC) and the University of Utah.

The <u>Matrix-Assisted Laser Desorption Ionization-Time of Flight-Mass Spectrometry (MALDI–TOF–MS)</u> is a variation of mass spectrometry that attempts to use a more gentle method of ionizing the suspect biological agent than pyrolysis to allow identification of the agent rather than just broad characterization.

<u>Chemical Biological Mass Spectrometer (CBMS)</u> uses a multistage process to analyze aerosols for biological content and categorize any biological constituents. The instrument first concentrates the aerosol, combusts or pyrolyzes it, then introduces the sample into a mass spectrometer for analysis. An on-board computer is used to analyze the mass spectra for patterns indicative of biological substances. The instrument is able to categorize biologicals as spores, cells, or toxins. Figure 5–10 shows an example of the CBMS from Bruker.

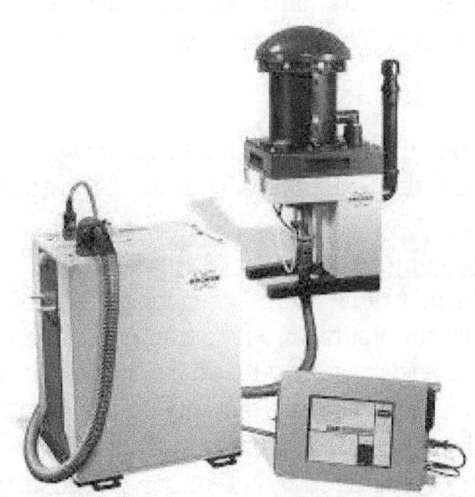

Figure 5–10. Chemical Biological Mass Spectrometer (CBMS), Bruker

5.1.4 Identifiers (Specific Identification Technologies)

Identifiers are those components/instruments that are able to identify the suspect biological agent to the species level (for cellular and viral agents) and toxin type. Specific identification technologies determine the presence of a specific biological agent by relying on the detection of a specific biomarker that is unique for that agent. Antibody-based identifiers are used for systems where speed and automation are required. Where time and manpower are available, gene-based systems start to take the lead.

The technologies that are used to specifically identify a biological agent are the most critical components of the detection architecture. These components have the widest variety of technologies and equipment available. Brief descriptions of several identifiers are included in sections 5.1.4.1 and 5.1.4.2.

5.1.4.1 Immunoassay Technologies

Immunoassay technologies detect and measure the highly specific binding of antigens (substances that are foreign to the body) with their corresponding antibodies by forming an antigen-antibody complex. In an immunoassay-based biological agent identification system, the presence of an analyte (agent) is detected and identified by relying on the specificity of the antigen-antibody binding event. The immunoassays are grouped into three categories: disposable matrix devices (tickets or kits), biosensors that use tag reagents to indirectly measure binding, and biosensors that do not require a tag (direct affinity assays). Each of these categories, along with examples of the corresponding technologies, is discussed below.

Disposable matrix devices: Disposable matrix devices are often referred to as tickets or kits. They usually involve dry reagents, which are reconstituted when a sample is added. There are one-step assay formats, as well as more complex formats involving multiple steps that are performed using one or more reagents. Ticket assays can be automated using instrumentation to perform the manual assay steps and provide a semiquantitative test readout. Rapid handheld assays with greater sensitivity, specificity, and reproducibility are under development for a wide range of bacterial agents and toxins. These assays have excellent stability characteristics, and test results are easy to obtain.

Typical ticket-based technologies include the Hand-Held Immunochromatographic Assays (HHAs), BTA™ Test Strips, and the Sensitive Membrane Antigen Rapid Test (SMART) system.

Hand-Held Immunochromatographic Assays (HHAs) are simple, one-time-use devices that are very similar to the urine test strips used in home pregnancy tests. There are currently 10 live agent assays in production, four simulants, and five trainers (only saline solution is needed to get positive results). These tests provide a yes/no response; however, a skilled observer can tell how much agent is present (semiquantitative measurement) by the degree of color change. HHAs are currently being used in virtually all fielded military biological detection systems, are in developmental systems, and are being used by a number of consequence management units. Their utility is due in large measure to their adaptability to automated readers as well as manual readers. Power is not required to use HHAs manually.

BTA™ Test Strips are detection strips that are manufactured by Tetracore LLC and distributed by Alexeter Technologies, LLC. The chemistry technique (lateral flow Immunochromatography) uses monoclonal antibodies that are specifically attracted to the target substance. When the level of the target substance is present in the sample above a certain concentration, the antibodies and target substance combine in the BTA™ Test Strip to form a reddish band that appears in a window. The test is positive if two colored lines appear. If only one colored line appears in the "C" Window, the test is negative. This technique provides fewer false positives in environmentally collected samples. Anthrax and ricin assays are available, with other assays in development. Figure 5–11 shows the Tetracore BTA™ Test Strip testing procedure.

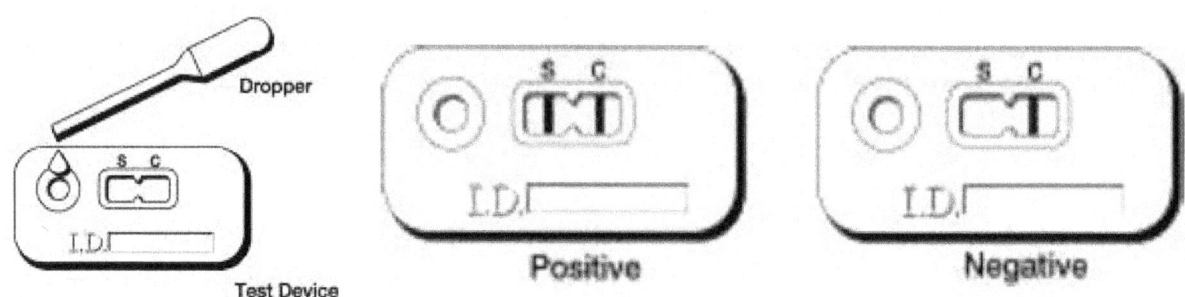

Figure 5–11. BTA™ Test Strip testing procedure, Tetracore, LCC

Sensitive Membrane Antigen Rapid Test (SMART) is a ticket-based system for detecting and identifying multiple analytes. The core chemistry approach detects antigens in the sample by immunofocusing colloidal gold-labeled reagents (leveled antibodies) and their corresponding antigens onto small membranes. Positive results (formation of a red dot) are detected by an instrument that measures the membrane reflectance. An automated ticket-based system can be used to perform the SMART immunoassays. Figure 5–12 shows an example of the NDI Smart Ticket, manufactured by New Horizons Diagnostics Corporation in Columbia, MD.

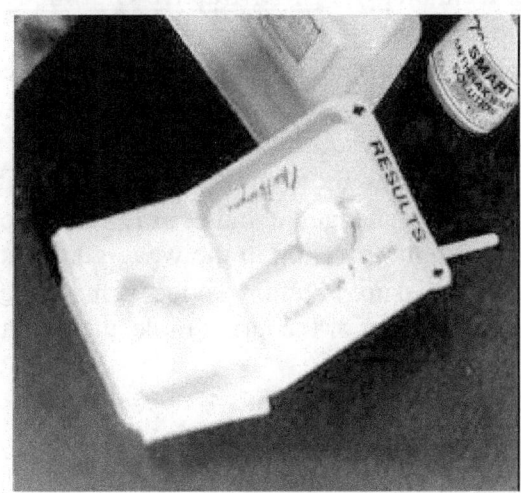

Figure 5–12. NDI Smart Ticket

Reagent Tag Biosensor Approaches: In this approach, biosensors integrate the sensing element (optical or electronic) with the biological coating to provide for a rapid, simple bio-analysis. In contrast with tickets, biosensors for biological agent detection consist of a sensing element, often enclosed in a flow cell, and an associated instrument for quantitative readout. A fluidics system is required to provide an automated, multi-analyte immunoassay to introduce the sample and one or more reagents into the sensor/flow cell during a test sequence. Biosensor-based assays are designed to be automated and often have an inherent capability for multi-analyte detection.

Reagent tag biosensor methods include fluorescent evanescent wave biosensor surface, electrochemiluminescence, Light Addressable Potentiometric Sensor (LAPS) Immunoassay, and latex particle agglutination/light scattering.

An example of fluorescent evanescent wave biosensor technology is the Fiber Optic Wave-Guide (FOWG). The FOWG uses antibody-coated fiber optic probes and a fluorescent "reporter" antibody to determine the presence of a suspect agent. If an agent is present in the aqueous solution circulating through the instrument, it will bind to the antibody on the probe. The instrument then circulates a second solution containing a fluorescent labeled antibody, which will also bind to the agent. The device then looks for the presence of the fluorescent tag on one of the probes.

No-Tag Reagent Biosensor Methods: Antigen-antibody binding is detected directly in no-tag reagent biosensor methods (i.e., direct affinity or homogeneous assays). Advantages to this type of assay include simplification of the analysis process (fewer steps, fewer components), minimized disposable fluid use (no need to carry tag reagent solutions), reuse of sensors after a negative test (minimal disposable use), and a smaller, lighter-weight instrument that consumes less power.

Examples of no-tag biosensor methods include interferometry, surface plasmon resonance, piezo-electric crystal microbalance, waveguide coupler, and electrical capacitance. The example of direct affinity no-tag biodetection technology is discussed in the following text. A device that

31

uses no-tag reagent biosensor technology is <u>Bi-Diffractive Grating Coupler (BDG)</u>, an optical transducer that is being developed by Battelle Memorial Institute and Hoffman-LaRoche. This device takes advantage of a phenomenon linked with one of the two components of a polarized light wave. Polarized light is divided into a transverse electric (TE) and transverse magnetic (TM) mode. The TM mode has an evanescent "tail" that moves with the light wave and above the medium (in this case, a plastic wave-guide that is coated with antibodies specific for a particular agent). The binding events change the index of refraction of the wave-guide surface layer, which alters the velocity of light traveling in the wave-guide through its evanescent field interaction. The optical property measured by this device, using optical interferometry, is the change in refractive index on the binding of the target molecule with the surface.

5.1.4.2 Nucleic Acid Amplification

Nucleic acid amplification may be used to help detect the presence of DNA or RNA of bacterial and viral biological agents (nucleic acid amplification cannot directly detect the presence of the toxins themselves). Samples for nucleic acid analysis can be obtained from field samples, from laboratory cultures, or from tissues of infected animals or humans. Polymerase chain reaction (PCR) is the most widely used method to amplify small quantities of DNA for analysis. Two examples of nucleic acid amplification are included in the following text.

The <u>Mini–PCR (Ten Chamber PCR)</u> is an instrument that has been developed by Lawrence Livermore National Laboratory (LLNL) and represents one of the first attempts to get gene-based identification technologies in a field-useable format. This device relies on a process called polymerase chain reaction (PCR) and a commercial chemistry called Taq-man®. A suspect sample is placed into a miniature thermal cycler that heats up and cools off very quickly and has miniature optics built into it; there are 10 of these mini-thermal cyclers in the 10 chamber device. In short, the instrument makes many copies of a particular gene segment of the suspect agent (if the agent is present), and as more copies are made, the more fluorescent light is generated by the Taq-man® process. The instrument is able to read the increase in light in near real time. This technology promises to be very sensitive and very specific.

The <u>LightCycler</u>™, developed by Idaho Technology, is a thermal cycler that uses a unique built-in fluorimetric detection system with specially developed fluorescent dyes, as well as Taq-man® technology, for on-line quantitation and amplification products. It is being manufactured under license by Roche Diagnostics. Figure 5–13 presents a picture of the LightCycler™.

The <u>Ruggedized Advanced Pathogen Identification Device (RAPID)</u>, from Idaho Technology, is a rugged, portable field instrument that integrates the LightCycler™ technology. The RAPID can run a reaction and automatically analyze the results in less than 30 min. Special software allows push button use of the RAPID, allowing for quick, safe, and accurate field identification of possibly dangerous pathogens. It is currently available for military field hospitals and law enforcement use. See Figure 5–14 for a picture of the RAPID.

Figure 5–13. Rapid LightCycler™,
Idaho Technology

Figure 5–14. RAPID, Idaho Technology

5.2 Standoff Technologies

Standoff systems are designed to detect and identify biological agents at a distance away from the aerosol/plume or from the detector system, before the agents reach the location of the system. Standoff systems do not utilize a trigger/cue, collector, or detector but use a bright light source such as a laser for detection of the biological agents.

Standoff technology uses the concept of detecting and measuring atmospheric properties by laser remote sensing or LIDAR, an acronym for light detection and ranging. In LIDAR, a short laser pulse is transmitted through the atmosphere, then a portion of that radiation is reflected back from a distant target or from atmospheric particles such as molecules, aerosols, clouds, or dust. All of these systems must be line-of-sight to the suspect biological agent event. Because LIDAR systems use light, which is composed of short wavelength energy, they are able to "see" the small aerosol particles characteristic of biological agent attacks (predominantly less than 20 μm in diameter). IR based LIDAR systems are able to see out to ranges of 30 km to 50 km as the atmosphere is fairly transparent to this wavelength of light. One limiting factor to standoff systems is the lack of availability of small, inexpensive high-power lasers. Several standoff instruments are identified below.

IR LIDARs cannot discriminate between biological and nonbiological aerosols; therefore, the remote detection of biological agents is best accomplished using a UV laser and the laser-induced fluorescence (LIF) technique. This results in an illuminated biological aerosol with a strong UV laser pulse that causes the biological agent to fluoresce. The fluorescence is red-shifted from the UV excitation frequency and detected in a longer wavelength UV band. The LIF system is more effective during low light or nighttime operations; the range is severely curtailed by the relative opacity of air to UV light and the high UV background during daylight hours.

Compact LIDAR is a system that has been in development at Soldier Biological and Chemical Command (SBCCOM) and Edgewood Chemical and Biological Center (ECBC) since 1996. The goal of the program is to develop a lightweight, ground-based standoff detection system that can track, calculate relative concentrations, and map potential biological aerosols. The system uses an IR laser system and cannot discriminate between biological and nonbiological aerosols.

Hybrid LIDAR is a system under development by the Electro Optics Organization Inc. (EOO) and Stanford Research Institute (SRI), under the sponsorship of the Defense Advanced Research Projects Agency (DARPA). The goal of this project is to develop a system that can be mounted on an unmanned aerial vehicle (UAV). The concept is that the UAV will loiter in an area, scanning for suspicious aerosols with its IR LIDAR component. When a suspect cloud is spotted, the UAV will move in close and interrogate the cloud for biological content using its ultraviolet (UV) component.

MIRELA is an IR LIDAR that is being collaboratively developed by SBCCOM and France. The system was originally developed for standoff detection of chemical clouds but is now being evaluated for bio-aerosol detection. This system cannot discriminate between biological and nonbiological aerosols.

MPL 1000 and MPL 2000 are commercially available IR LIDAR systems (manufactured by Science and Engineering Services, Inc.-SESI) originally developed in collaboration with NASA-Goddard Space Flight Center for monitoring atmospheric cloud and aerosol structures. NASA and DOE now have over a dozen MPL instruments in routine use at research sites. These instruments cannot discriminate between biological and nonbiological aerosols.

Of the standoff detection systems discussed, the MPL 1000 is the closest to being a fieldable standoff detection system. The system is already in production and is fairly lightweight and rugged. This system, as is true with all the systems, requires additional time to develop its detection algorithm. All of the standoff detection systems described require manual interpretation of raw data.

The Long-Range Biological Standoff Detection System (LR-BSDS) can detect aerosol clouds up to 30 km from the detector from an airborne platform, specifically a helicopter. This system uses pulsed laser beams in the near-IR regime of the optical spectrum (1 μm) to detect these clouds. However, since only aerosol clouds are detected, there is no biological discrimination to distinguish these clouds from other clouds, such as dust clouds. See Figure 5–15 for an example of a long-range detector system.

Figure 5–15. Long-Range Biological
Standoff Detection System (LIDARS)

5.3 Passive Standoff Technologies

Passive standoff detection systems rely on the background electromagnetic energy present in the environment for detection of biological agents. Typically, these systems look at the mid-IR (3 μ to 5 μ) or far-IR (8 μ to 12 μ) region of the spectrum for agent signatures. Currently researchers are investigating the utility of IR spectroscopy for detection and identification of biological agents. While bio-aerosols have been visualized by IR systems immediately after dissemination, they quickly loose that signature and become invisible to current passive systems. Systems such as the M21 Remote Sensing Chemical Agent Alarm (RSCAAL) and Joint Service Lightweight Standoff Chemical Agent Detector (JSLSCAD) have been used in attempts to detect biological agents with little success.

6. HOW TO PREPARE FOR A BIOLOGICAL INCIDENT

This section provides emergency first responders and other interested organizations with information on what actions an emergency first responder should take in the case of a biological incident. It has information on Federal and State programs for support, crisis management, and functional tasks during a terrorist attack.

6.1 Federal and State Programs for Support

As outlined in previous sections of this guide, biological detection equipment is mainly in the developmental phase. Because of this, there is a limited number of commercially available instruments; what is available is costly and has limited utility. Without equipment to detect and identify a biological agent, emergency first responders must turn to existing State and Federal organizations for support.

A number of State and Federal agencies are working throughout the country to set up standards for operations during a terrorist attack involving biological, chemical, or nuclear weapons of mass destruction. The Centers for Disease Control and Prevention (CDC) is coordinating a nationwide program called the National Laboratory System (NLS) to provide communication, coordination, and testing capacity required to effectively detect and report disease outbreaks and exposures (see app. B, ref. 1). The goal of the NLS is to integrate the reporting and response of disease outbreaks and/or terrorist bioweapon attacks. The system will integrate Federal, State, and local public health laboratories, as well as hospital, independent, and physicians' laboratories, for monitoring the population for an outbreak of disease. Through the NLS, the CDC provides private and State public health laboratories with information, analytical methods, and analytical reagents for analysis of biological agents. The CDC also sponsors the Laboratory Response Network (LRN) through the Association of Public Health Laboratories (see app. B, ref. 2). The LRN is focused on educating laboratories on the methods needed to test for biological agents.

The emergency first responder must recognize that while public health laboratories and supporting clinical laboratories have the capability to detect and identify possible biological agents, these tests are not field deployable. The detection methods used are laboratory-based systems and should not be confused with field-based systems described in earlier portions of this guide. Generally, the laboratory-based systems are slower than field systems, but the laboratory-based systems exhibit greater selectivity and versatility than field-based systems. It should also be recognized that different laboratories have different capabilities.

The CDC uses a four-level categorization of laboratory responsibilities for detection and identification of a biological agent. The laboratories are categorized as Level A, Level B, Level C, and Level D laboratories.

- Level A laboratories focus on early detection of intentional dissemination of biological agents. They are mostly composed of microbiology laboratories that conduct primary clinical testing, such as hospital and independent laboratories. Level A laboratories are responsible for ruling out the presence of pathogenic organisms and forwarding suspicious and potentially dangerous organisms to laboratories capable of identifying the organisms.

- Level B laboratories focus on testing for specific agents and forwarding organisms or specimens to higher level biocontaminant laboratories.
- Level C laboratories focus on advanced and specialized testing for rapid identification of biological agents.
- Level D laboratories focus on diagnosis of rare and dangerous biological agents.

First responders will generally only have to deal with Level A laboratories.

6.2 Crisis Management in a Terrorist Attack

Crisis management must be integrated and managed under an overall unified command structure during a terrorist attack (see app. B, ref. 3). Crisis management for a terrorist attack using biological agents consists of public health monitoring, surveillance, detection, and reporting the use of a biological weapon of mass destruction (WMD).

Emergency first responders (fire and rescue) will be involved in the early stages of crisis management, primarily the reporting of the possible use of a biological weapon. For this reason, emergency first responders need to have an emergency response plan in place for any possible biological (as well as chemical and radiological) incident. Therefore, it is strongly recommended that emergency first responders plan their response to a biological (as well as chemical and radiological) incident well in advance.

A recent report in the State of Maryland entitled "Maryland Health and Medical System Preparedness and Response Plan—Weapons of Mass Destruction, Work Plan," suggests that the response to an incident be coordinated through local, State, and Federal channels to ensure complete integration of the local response to any such incident (see app. B, ref. 3). The State of Maryland recommends coordination with the State police, the State public health department/laboratories, and the Federal Bureau of Investigation (FBI). It is stressed that these are the recommendations of the State of Maryland; recommendations may be different for each State. Therefore, it is essential that the first responder contact local and State officials in order to coordinate a response to a biological agent incident.

6.3 Functional Tasks During a Terrorist Attack

In the event of a terrorist attack using biological agents, each supporting agency has different functional tasks that must be carried out. Local fire and rescue service's functional tasks state that, "The Fire Chief, or first ranking officer on the scene, will be the initial incident commander for single point source incidents and must make initial determinations on tactical responses and additional support …." (see app. B, ref. 3). Local officials must plan ahead for this contingency by providing senior officers of the fire and police departments with education and training on the identification of biological (and chemical or nuclear) incident.

Once it is determined that the event is a result of a release of a biological agent (either by a terrorist or accidental), the appropriate authorities must be contacted. In the State of Maryland, first responders should contact the Maryland State Police who are to "assist with early detection and monitoring activities by notifying the Department of Health and Mental Hygiene and the Local Health Officer of threats, credible threats, impending events, or actual terrorist acts that may produce casualties" (see app. B, ref. 3). Each first responder unit must first determine the response chain for their particular State. In this way, the first responder is integrated into the overall response to a biological (and chemical or nuclear) incident.

7. SUMMARY

An Introduction to Biological Agent Detection Equipment for Emergency First Responders was developed to provide information to the emergency first responder community and aid their understanding of biological agent detection equipment. Information included in the guide focuses on biological agents, challenges of detection, components of detection, and the basic technologies that have been or are being considered in the research and development (R&D) of biological agent detection equipment.

The guide identifies a number of biological agent detection technologies and some equipment associated with the technologies.[5] It is important to note that the equipment referenced is not all inclusive with what is currently available or currently being tested. While some equipment is commercially available, most is not (a notable exception is Tetracore test strips for biological agents).[6] It is also important to realize that biological detection equipment is limited with respect to biological agents detected as well as operational conditions. Because of this, *An Introduction to Biological Agent Detection Equipment for Emergency First Responders* was written to serve the first responder community as a guide to the status of biological agent detection.

Because commercially available biological agent detection equipment prices range from tens to hundreds of thousands of dollars, it is obvious that R&D efforts will have to continue.[7] These efforts will focus on lowering equipment costs while improving equipment sensitivity and selectivity. As new equipment and technologies emerge, and more importantly for the first responders, as equipment becomes commercially available, this guide will be updated.

Because of the lack of affordable detection equipment for biological agents, first responders must integrate their response into the overall national effort. This national effort is being developed by the CDC as well as the FBI and includes the development of analytical assets at State health laboratories for detecting biological agents. The link from the first responders to the national response effort is most likely the State police and the State public health laboratories. However, this plan is based on the State of Maryland plan and may be different for each State. Therefore, in developing a response plan for biological weapons, it is recommended that first responders contact their State police to determine if a standard operating procedure (SOP) for a terrorist attack using biological, chemical, or nuclear WMD exists. It is also suggested that prior to an event involving a biological WMD, first responders contact the nearest public health laboratory to determine points of contact. Appendix B lists the phone numbers for public health laboratories in most States, as well as the Association of Public Health Laboratories (a nonprofit association working to actively promote the interest of public health laboratories), and internet addresses for the Association of Public Health Laboratories, CDC, and State Public Health Laboratory home pages (see app. B, ref. 2, 4, and 5).

---

[5] It is critical to understand that reference to these technologies and equipment by trade name, trademark, manufacturer, or otherwise does not necessarily constitute or imply its endorsement, recommendations, or favoring by the United States Government.

[6] For example, immunoassay tickets are relatively inexpensive; however, the antibodies that are required for identification of the biological agents are not commercially available.

APPENDIX A—REFERENCES

APPENDIX A—REFERENCES

1. John A. Barrett, Gregory W. Bowen, Scott M. Golly, Christopher Hawley, William M. Jackson, Leo Laughlin, Megan E. Lynch, *Assessment of Biological Agent Detection Equipment for Emergency Responders*, June 1, 1998. Chemical Biological Information Analysis Center (CBIAC), P.O. Box 196, Gunpowder, MD 21010-0196.

2. *Chemical and Biological Terrorism: Research and Development to Improve Civilian Medical Response to Chemical and Biological Terrorism Incidents*, National Academy of Sciences, 1999. National Academy Press, 2101 Constitution Avenue, N.W., Box 285, Washington, DC 20055.

3. John A. Barrett, Gregory W. Bowen, Scott M. Golly, Christopher Hawley, William M. Jackson, Leo Laughlin, Megan E. Lynch, *Final Report on the Assessment of Biological Agent Detection Equipment for Emergency Responders*, U.S. Army Chemical and Biological Defense Command (CBDCOM), June 1, 1998. CBIAC, P.O. Box 196, Gunpowder, MD 21010-0196.

4. *Assessment of Biological Warfare Detection (CD)* Joint Program Office for Bio-Defense, Skyline #2, 5203 Leesburg Pike, Suite 1609, Falls Church, VA 22041-3203, September 13, 1999.

5. *State of the Art Report on Biodetection Technologies*, July 1995. CBIAC, P.O. Box 196, Gunpowder, MD 21010-0196.

6. B. Newman, *"Opening the Case of the Poison Umbrella,"* The Wall Street Journal, May 24, 1991. E-mail address: http://chiron.valdosta.edu/rgoddard/biol4900/corbett/corbett.htm .

APPENDIX B—CONTACT INFORMATION
FOR FIRST RESPONDERS

Telephone Numbers for State Public Health Laboratories

Association of Public Health Labs	202–822–5227
Alaska	907–269–7942
Arizona	602–542–1194
California	510–540–2408
Colorado	303–692–3289
Connecticut	860–509–8540
Florida	850–245–4401 e-mail Bill Dart (Bill_Dart@doh.state.fl.us)
Georgia	404–327–7900
Idaho	208-334–5939
Illinois	217–782–4977
Indiana	317–233–8006
Kansas	785–296–1620
Louisiana	504–568–5375
Maine	207–287–2727
Massachusetts	617–983–6200
Michigan	517–335–8063
Minnesota	651–215–5800
Missouri	573–751–0633
Nebraska	402–552–3350
New Jersey	609–292–0430
New Mexico	505–841–2500
New York	716–898–6100
North Carolina	919–733–7834
Ohio	888–634–5227
Oklahoma	405–271–5070
Oregon	503–229–5882
South Dakota	800–738–2301
Tennessee	615–262–6300
Texas	512–458–7228 512–458–7676
Utah	801–538–6128
Vermont	802–863–7240 800–640–4374
Virginia	804–786–7905
Washington	206–361–2800
West Virginia	304–558–3530
Wisconsin	888–494–4324
Wyoming	307–777–7431

Suggested Websites and Addresses for More Complete Information

1. National Laboratory System (NLS) Division of Laboratory Systems (DLS): http://www.phppo.cdc.gov/mlp/nls.asp .
2. Association of Public Health Laboratories: http://www.aphl.org/ .
3. Maryland Health and Medical System Preparedness and Response Plan—Weapons of Mass Destruction, Work Plan, James R. Stanton, Maryland Institute for Emergency Medical Services Systems (410-706-0415), May 2000.
4. Center for Disease Control: http://www.cdc.gov/ .
5. Public Health Laboratory listings: http://www.phppo.cdc.gov/DLS/links/links_phl.asp .

ABOUT THE LAW ENFORCEMENT AND CORRECTIONS STANDARDS AND TESTING PROGRAM

The Law Enforcement and Corrections Standards and Testing Program is sponsored by the Office of Science and Technology of the National Institute of Justice (NIJ), U.S. Department of Justice. The program responds to the mandate of the Justice System Improvement Act of 1979, directed NIJ to encourage research and development to improve the criminal justice system and to disseminate the results to Federal, State, and local agencies.

The Law Enforcement and Corrections Standards and Testing Program is an applied research effort that determines the technological needs of justice system agencies, sets minimum performance standards for specific devices, tests commercially available equipment against those standards, and disseminates the standards and the test results to criminal justice agencies nationally and internationally.

The program operates through:

The *Law Enforcement and Corrections Technology Advisory Council* (LECTAC), consisting of nationally recognized criminal justice practitioners from Federal, State, and local agencies, which assesses technological needs and sets priorities for research programs and items to be evaluated and tested.

The *Office of Law Enforcement Standards* (OLES) at the National Institute of Standards and Technology, which develops voluntary national performance standards for compliance testing to ensure that individual items of equipment are suitable for use by criminal justice agencies. The standards are based upon laboratory testing and evaluation of representative samples of each item of equipment to determine the key attributes, develop test methods, and establish minimum performance requirements for each essential attribute. In addition to the highly technical standards, OLES also produces technical reports and user guidelines that explain in nontechnical terms the capabilities of available equipment.

The *National Law Enforcement and Corrections Technology Center* (NLECTC), operated by a grantee, which supervises a national compliance testing program conducted by independent laboratories. The standards developed by OLES serve as performance benchmarks against which commercial equipment is measured. The facilities, personnel, and testing capabilities of the independent laboratories are evaluated by OLES prior to testing each item of equipment, and OLES helps the NLECTC staff review and analyze data. Test results are published in Equipment Performance Reports designed to help justice system procurement officials make informed purchasing decisions.

Publications are available at no charge through the National Law Enforcement and Corrections Technology Center. Some documents are also available online through the Internet/World Wide Web. To request a document or additional information, call 800–248–2742 or 301–519–5060, or write:

National Law Enforcement and Corrections Technology Center
P.O. Box 1160
Rockville, MD 20849–1160
E-Mail: *asknlectc@nlectc.org*
World Wide Web address: *http://www.nlectc.org*

This document is not intended to create, does not create, and may not be relied upon to create any rights, substantive or procedural, enforceable at law by any party in any matter civil or criminal.

Opinions or points of view expressed in this document represent a consensus of the authors and do not represent the official position or policies of the U.S. Department of Justice. The products and manufacturers discussed in this document are presented for informational purposes only and do not constitute product approval or endorsement by the U.S. Department of Justice.

The National Institute of Justice is a component of the Office of Justice Programs, which also includes the Bureau of Justice Assistance, the Bureau of Justice Statistics, the Office of Juvenile Justice and Delinquency Prevention, and the Office for Victims of Crime.